How Cool Are

PENGUINS

How Cool Are Penguins

Edited by Karen L. Tucker, CommaQueenEditing.com

Paperback ISBN: 978-1-952924-01-9

Dedication

This book is dedicated to all children
who have a love of nature
and the world around them.

Acknowledgment

I gratefully acknowledge the loving support of my husband and family without whose encouragement this would not have been possible. A special thank you to my daughter, Jen, for her help and creative ideas and my exercise ladies, who, although grandmothers themselves, graciously and patiently allowed me to read to them as though they were small children.

What is a penguin?

A penguin is a bird that swims but does not fly. I bet you think that's silly! Everybody knows that birds fly.

Not penguins! These birds are different.

They like to swim. Do you?

Where do penguins live?

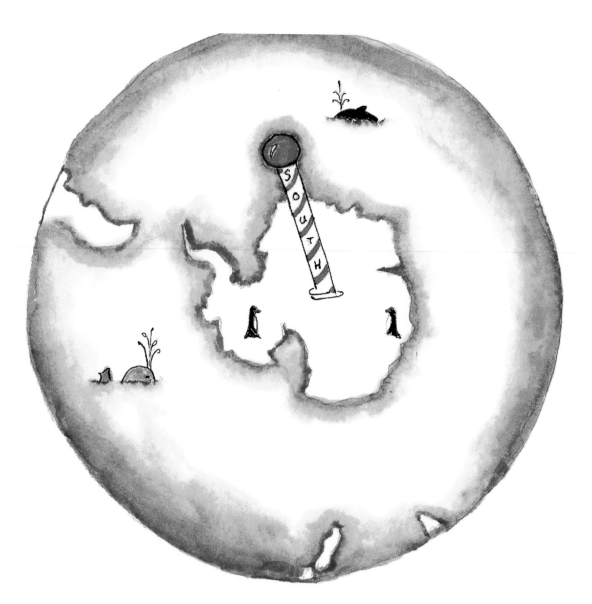

Wild penguins are found near the South Pole. Some like the very, VERY cold Antarctic region.

Others like the warmer areas near Argentina, Australia and other islands around the South Pole.

All penguins like cold water. Do you?

What do penguins like to eat?

Many birds like berries, seeds and even worms. Not penguins!
They love a good seafood meal.

They must dive into the cold waters and search for fish.
Yum! They dive into the water all skinny and come back with fat
little bellies!

Penguins love fish. Do you?

Do penguins sleep?

Of course! Penguins take naps for a few minutes or
a few hours. They sleep longest at night. Just like you and me.

Penguins can sleep lying down on their bellies. They sleep while sitting. They can even sleep standing up!

Penguins sometimes sleep on rocks! Can you?

How are baby penguins born?

Baby penguins are hatched from eggs. The mommy penguin will lay at least one egg.

Both parents take turns caring for their egg. While one protects the egg and keeps it warm, the other goes off to eat.

I think that little egg is happy. Don't you?

This can be hard work! Emperor penguins
live on the Antarctic ice. Brrrr!!

They must carefully balance their egg on the tops of their feet.
They cover their egg with their belly to keep the egg warm. The
egg must NOT touch the ice!

What do penguins look like?

Short body feathers

Long tail feathers

Like all birds, penguins have feathers. Mostly their feathers
are black and white, but some are blue.

Baby penguins are fluffy and gray or brown and white. There are 17 different kinds of penguins. All of them are adorable!

I want to learn all about penguins! Do you?

Let's look at some different kinds of penguins.

The Little, or Blue, penguins are the smallest. They are about a foot tall and, of course, are blue!

The Emperor penguins are the biggest.
They are almost 4 feet tall.

How tall are you?

The Adelie penguins aren't very big, but they are curious, and they are fierce.

Chinstrap penguins look like they are wearing a black helmet.

Gentoo penguins have bright red-orange beaks and peach-colored feet. They have white feathers behind their eyes that look like earmuffs.

Different penguins have different "hats." Do you?

Some penguins have long feathers that stick out on their heads. These are called crests.

Some crests are white. Some crests are black. Some are even yellow or orange! This makes them look rather fancy.

Just like us, penguins don't all look the same. Some are tall. Some are short. The color of their feathers is different. BUT, like you, all penguins are awesome!

I think penguins are cool! Do you?

No matter what penguins look like, they all move the same.

In the oceans, they are graceful. They are all fast.

On the land, they trip over things.
They bump into things. And penguins ...

waddle! Do you?

Would you like to be a penguin for a day? You would swim. You would eat lots of fish. You would sleep under the stars.

Do you think that sounds like fun? I do!

Penguins are the coolest birds. They can swim, eat fish AND waddle. Now YOU know something about penguins!

If you ever meet one, say hi for me!

Are you curious to know more about penguins? Here are a few fun facts:

- Male penguins will sometimes give female penguins rocks to impress them. The females will use these rocks to build their nest.

- A group of penguins in the water is called a raft.

- To help them keep warm, penguins have a gland near the base of their tail that provides a waterproof oil. For several hours per day, penguins work to cover their feathers with this oil, especially before swimming.

- Penguins can drink sea water.

- A penguin's black-and-white coloring serves to camouflage them while swimming. From above, the black plumage on their back is hard to see. From below, the white plumage looks like the sun reflecting off the surface of the water.

- To get back on land, some smaller penguins will jump 6 to 9 feet into the air by speedily swimming to the surface.

- There are fossils that indicate an ancient penguin stood 5' 10". Can you imagine being eye to eye with such a big bird?

Sources: Caroline Picard, "30 Absolutely Delightful Facts You Never Knew About Penguins," Good Housekeeping, Jan. 17, 2020, www.goodhousekeeping.com/life/g19844807/penguin-facts/.

"10 Cool Facts About Penguins," City of Albuquerque, accessed Nov. 24, 2020, www.cabq.gov/culturalservices/biopark/news/10-cool-facts-about-penguins/.

Science Kids, "Fun Facts About Penguins!" Cool Australia, accessed Nov. 24, 2020, www.coolaustralia.org/fun-facts-about-penguins/.

Made in the USA
Monee, IL
15 December 2020